A field guide to
Spring

A Field Guide to Spring © 2024 Thames & Hudson Ltd, London
Text © 2024 Gabby Dawnay
Illustrations © 2024 Dorien Brouwers
Forest School consultant: Louise Black

First published in the United States of America in 2024 by Thames & Hudson Inc.,
500 Fifth Avenue, New York, New York 10110

Library of Congress Control Number 2023939922

ISBN 978-0-500-65351-7

Printed and bound in China by Toppan Leefung Printing Limited

MIX
Paper from
responsible sources
FSC® C104723

Be the first to know about our new releases,
exclusive content and author events by visiting
thamesandhudson.com
thamesandhudsonusa.com
thamesandhudson.com.au

A field guide to
Spring

Gabby Dawnay

Illustrated by Dorien Brouwers

t&h

what's inside?

wild by nature

Welcome to spring

Let's learn all about spring by spending time in the wild. Because the more you spend time with nature, the better friends you'll become.

You will find that by being CURIOUS about nature, CREATIVE in nature, and KIND to nature you'll quickly become a nature expert. There's so much fun to be had just by playing, talking, asking questions, and getting creative in the wild. So what are you waiting for?

HOW TO MAKE NATURE YOUR FRIEND

BE CURIOUS

What questions spring to mind?
What do you know?
What don't you know?
How can you find out more?

BE CREATIVE

Take the time to look closely at nature.
What colors, shapes, and patterns do you notice?
What connections can you find?

BE KIND

Imagine the world from a bug's point of view . . .
. . . or from a bird's.
How old is this tree and what has it seen?
If you were a flower, would you want to be picked?

LEARN

Discover more
about nature.

FEEL

How do you
feel in nature?

BE

Be a part
of nature.

sensing
spring

Noticing nature's changes

The signs of spring appear very slowly. But if you use your SENSES, you will discover nature changing right in front of you.

Go for a walk and find a tree that is away from noisy roads and playgrounds. Stand with your back to it.

 SMELL — Close your eyes and take a deep breath. What can you smell?

 LISTEN — Stand very still and listen to the sounds. What can you hear?

 LOOK — Open your eyes slowly, as if you've just woken up. What can you see?

 TOUCH — Crouch down and touch the ground. What can you feel?

TASTE — Stretch up to the sky and lick your lips. What can you taste?

Whether you live in a busy city or quiet countryside, you can use your super senses to spot the changes in nature as they happen. Have you noticed any of these signs lately?

THE SIGNS OF SPRING

BUGS emerging from a sleepy state

BLOSSOMS bursting into bloom

BIRDS singing after a long, cold winter

BABY ANIMALS bringing new life

RAIN showers and rainbows

POND LIFE stirring

SEEDLINGS sprouting

WARMTH in the weather

LONGER DAYS and shorter nights

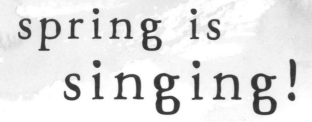

spring is singing!

A poem to read under a tree

Something's stirring underneath
as buds appear for every leaf.
The sleeping bulbs are slowly rooting,
creeping stalks and branches shooting.

In the water there are lots
of tiny, slimy, bubble-dots . . .
Twitching tails and legs are showing,
watch the inky wrigglers growing!

Here's a warm and feathered nest
where tiny eggs together rest.
Until a wobble, then a crack
and busy ducklings start to quack!

Hello tadpoles, hello chicks,
hello green and sprouting sticks!

Hello spring—it's time to heat
the sleepy earth beneath our feet.
Days are longer, mornings lighter—
even sunshine seems much brighter!

Hello grass and hello flowers,
hello sun and springtime showers!

Wake up garden! After snow
your leafy beds begin to grow . . .
And from the winter's icy rain
the whole of nature wakes again!

Hello singing in the air—
Spring is springing everywhere!

What signs of
spring does the
poem mention?

little
seedlings

How seeds turn into plants

Some of the first things in nature to wake up after a long winter are seeds. They lie still under the earth throughout the colder months. When the weather warms up in spring, they are ready to start growing.

How does a seed grow?

1. First a seed sends roots down into the ground.

2. Then it pushes a leafy bud up through the surface of the soil.

MEASURE the height of a seedling with a ruler at the same time every week. How tall did it grow in one week? What will it become?

TIP *Be careful not to touch or step on seedlings! They are young and tender, like newborn babies.*

3. Next the seedling's stalk grows and its leaves unfurl. A seedling grows into a plant using energy from the sun.

A seed turns into a seedling during the spring. This process is called **germination**.

scattering
seeds

Make your own seed balls

Spring is the perfect time to plant wildflower seeds so that they will bloom in summer. Seed balls are a fun and easy way to plant flowers.

WHAT YOU NEED:

- a mixing bowl
- wildflower seeds
- peat-free compost
- powdered clay
  (found in craft stores)
- water
- a tray or a sheet
  of newspaper

TIP *If you can't find powdered clay, use plain flour instead.*

1. Add 1 handful of seeds, 5 handfuls of compost, and 3 of clay powder to your bowl and mix together.

2. Slowly mix in water until your mixture looks like a sticky dough.

3. Roll clumps of the mixture in your hands to form firm balls.

4. Leave your seed balls to dry for a few days on a tray or a sheet of old newspaper.

TIP *Most wildflowers should be planted between March and May. Check the seed packet to find the best time to make your seed balls.*

5. Now it's time to get planting! Have fun throwing your balls into flowerbeds in your garden.

📖 LEARN Not only are wildflowers beautiful to look at, they also provide homes and food for lots of different insects.

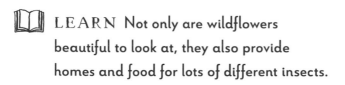

budding
blossom

When trees and plants bloom

See buds bursting into life! There are pale pink, white,
and lime-green blossoms all over the trees.

Many blossoms are the flowers of fruit trees. Cherries,
plums, peaches, apples, pears, and apricots all begin
as delicate blooms. Then a week or two later, gusts
of wind scatter the petals, covering the ground in
a carpet of pink and white confetti.

 Can you SMELL the scent of blossoms in the air?

Can you see any trees with tiny, silvery buds on them? They are more like kitten tails than flowers! These fluffy blossoms are called pussy willow. They are a type of **catkin** that grows on willow trees and they are usually the first blooms to appear in spring.

TOUCH them. What do they feel like?

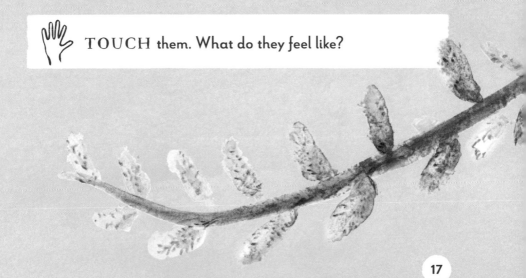

17

blooming
beautifully

How to identify spring flowers

BLUEBELLS
- Little bell-shaped flowers
- Grows in woodland
- Bendy stem
- Bluish-purple flowers

DAFFODIL
- Yellow or white flower
- Trumpet-shaped center
- Six outer petals
- Long, thick stem

TULIPS

- Large, cup-shaped flowers
- Tall, straight stem
- Come in lots of different colors
- Large leaves

 LOOK for spring blooms in wooded areas and meadows, as well as in towns and gardens.
What color is the flower?
What shape are the petals?
What is the stem like?
What shape are the leaves?

HYACINTH

- A cluster or spike of star-shaped flowers
- Sweet smelling
- Blue, pink, or white flowers
- Thick, straight stem

pond life

From tadpole to frog

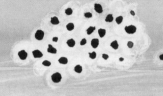

Do you have a pond near where you live? Can you see any **frogspawn** in it? Don't touch it—but imagine what it would feel like! What words would you use to describe it?

Visit the pond each day. What's happening to the frogspawn? Take a notepad and write down the day when . . .

1. Frogspawn first appears.

5. . . . and then their front ones.

6. Are they tiny froglets yet?

2. Little tails form inside the eggs.

3. Tadpoles hatch and start to swim.

4. Tadpoles grow their back legs . . .

Can you draw them at every stage?

7. Frogs lose their tails.

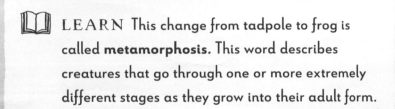

Once they have grown up, the frogs hop out of the pond! How long does this transformation take?

21

find an amphibian

How to identify frogs, toads, and newts

Frogs, toads, and newts all belong to a group of animals called **amphibians**. They can live on land and in water.

FROG

- Smooth, wet-looking skin
- Long legs
- Leap and hop on land
- Like to stay close to water

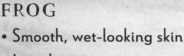 **LOOK** for eggs in the shallows of ponds and lakes.

TOAD
- Dry, bumpy skin
- Short legs
- Crawl around on land
- Happy on dry land

NEWT
- Long, thin body
- Long tail
- Thin legs
- Small head

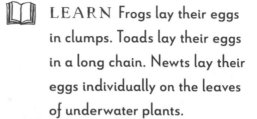

 LEARN Frogs lay their eggs in clumps. Toads lay their eggs in a long chain. Newts lay their eggs individually on the leaves of underwater plants.

pond
dipping

What's in the water?

Perhaps there's a pond in the park with a bloom
of bright green weed covering its inky surface? Or a
swampy patch of water in the middle of the woods?

> **BREATHE IN** the lovely,
> weedy, reedy stink of mossy,
> mushy, pondy dampness.

In even a tiny patch of water, if conditions are
right, belching frogs produce their beautiful
gelatinous frogspawn.

Plants covering the water—such as duckweed,
water lilies, marsh marigolds, and water
violets—help to create the perfect breeding
ground for frogs and lots of other wildlife.

Time for some pond life investigation!

Use your cup to transfer some pond water into the shallow dish. Then dip your net in the pond, scoop, and carefully empty the contents into the dish . . . Did you get splashed?

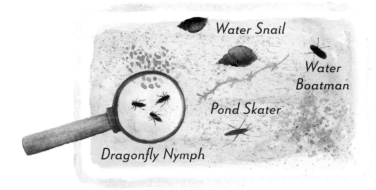

Water Snail

Water Boatman

Pond Skater

Dragonfly Nymph

👁 **LOOK** with your magnifying glass . . . What can you see?

Remember to return everything carefully to the pond afterward. Record what you found in a notebook or in your memory. Why not draw a picture?

time
to nest

Birds and their babies

As the weather gets milder, it's time for many birds to build a nest. Lots of birds live near water. So, while you're at the pond, look out for mallard ducks and moorhens, geese and swans. Perhaps a heron watches from a distance, standing on one leg in the water.

Female DUCKS build their nests from grasses and leaves and sometimes line them with feathers plucked from their chests.

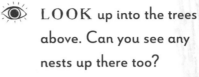

👁 LOOK up into the trees above. Can you see any nests up there too?

These **waterbirds** build their nests in or by water, at ground level. They make them a cozy, safe place to lay their eggs, just like the birds that nest in trees.

SWANS and GEESE return to the same pond or river year after year. They build huge nests using twigs, leaves, and vegetation.

👂 LISTEN Ponds, rivers, and **wetlands** can be noisy places in spring! Can you hear the different waterbirds calling? What sounds do they make?

27

who laid that?

How to identify birds' eggs

Have you ever stumbled across pieces of eggshell while out and about? They probably belonged to a baby bird that hatched. The colors, shape, and size of an egg can help us work out what type of bird it came from.

PIGEON
- White with no markings
- About 1 x 1.5 inches

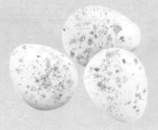

BLUE TIT
- Cream with brown speckles
- About 0.5 x 0.6 inches

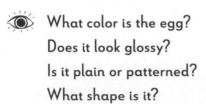

What color is the egg?
Does it look glossy?
Is it plain or patterned?
What shape is it?

BLACKBIRD
- Blue with pale brown speckles
- About 0.8 x 1.1 inches

PHEASANT
- Greenish-brown with no markings
- About 1.4 x 1.7 inches

HOUSE SPARROW
- White or blueish-white with thick brown or gray speckles
- About 0.8 x 1.6 inches

STARLING
- Blue with no markings
- About 0.8 x 1.1 inches

 LEAVE NESTS TO REST You should never touch eggs in a nest and always be careful not to disturb nesting birds.

brilliant builders

Build your own bird's nest

Many birds create beautiful, intricate nests using only their beaks! Try your hand at making your own nest from natural materials that a bird might use.

Go on a walk to collect materials for your nest.

LOOK FOR:

- twigs or vines (the bendier the better!)
- dried grass
- leaves
- moss
- feathers
- mud

1. Start by twisting and tying some bendy twigs or vines together into a circle. Build out from there, weaving in more twigs to make a nest shape.

While you're on your walk, LOOK out for a real bird's nest in bushes or trees. Don't touch or disturb it but look closely.

What materials is it made from?

Can you tell how it was made?

What type of bird might have made it?

2. Poke other natural materials, such as grass, leaves, and feathers into the gaps in your nest.

3. Fill the nest with moss, dried grass, or feathers to make a soft cushion for eggs.

TIP *Give birds a hand with their own nest building by leaving leftover natural materials in easy-to-find places for them to collect.*

bouncing
baby animals

Signs of new life

Many animals have their babies in spring.
Why do you think they choose this time of year?

Remember, the temperature rises in spring and the
days become longer. This means animals have more time
to find food for their young and the ground is softer and
easier to dig into for tasty grubs. There are also lots of
yummy new shoots and fresh green leaves to munch.

There is new life all
around us in spring!

SQUIRREL KITS emerge from their treetop nest, called a "drey," at 7 weeks old. They still drink their mother's milk, but by 10 weeks they begin to **forage** for nuts and seeds.

FAWNS stay close to mother deer in the cool woodland and drink her milk. Their spotted backs help them **camouflage** in the shadows.

FOX CUBS tumble and play together. They will eat whatever their parents find for them. In the city, they scavenge for scraps of food. In the forest, they'll hunt for birds, small **mammals**, and bugs.

👁 LOOK for tiny pawprints and hoofprints. Which animals made them?

frolic
in the fields

Feeding the kids

Fields in springtime are full of life! If you visit, you might see . . .

LAMBS skipping for joy when the sun comes out! They gambol and play around the mother sheep.

CALVES stroll along with their herd in a grassy, muddy meadow. The mother cow is never far away.

LISTEN for sounds of new life.
What noise do lambs make?
What noise do calves make?
What noise do foals make?

All these mammals drink their mother's
milk, just like human babies.

How many other animals can
you think of that are born
in spring?

FOALS at first wobble on
bandy legs. They run and
keep close to mother horse.

RABBIT KITTENS stay snug in
the underground burrow while
their mother munches on tender
spring grass and shoots.

let the
sun shine

Time for warmer weather

The sun shines a little more. It rises earlier
and sets later. With light peeping through the
curtains, do you wake up a little earlier?

 LISTEN Can you hear birds singing early in the
morning? That's the dawn chorus! If you listen hard
enough, maybe you'll hear the different songs they
are singing . . .

Softly, softly, sunshine thaws the earth to wake what sleeps
beneath the surface. The hard ground softens underfoot.

Take your shoes and socks off and run!
How does the grass FEEL under your feet?

LOOK Can you see any snowdrops or crocuses poking
through the earth? Careful not to squash the new life!

LISTEN Do you hear the bees buzzing?
They are excited to be visiting the new flowers!

37

glowing
warmth

Why the weather gets warmer

In spring:

- Our planet Earth spins closer to the sun.
- The sun rises earlier in the morning and sets later in the evening.
- The weather changes from gray skies to sunny days.
- The ground starts to warm up.

Stand in the sunshine and get
a friend to trace your shadow.

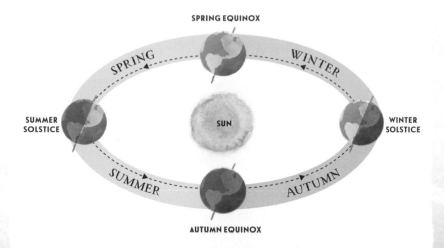

SPRING EQUINOX

SPRING

WINTER

SUMMER SOLSTICE

SUN

WINTER SOLSTICE

SUMMER

AUTUMN

AUTUMN EQUINOX

Earth tilts toward the sun and the natural world awakens from its long snooze through the cold winter months.

Spring is measured as the period of time between the spring **equinox** and the summer **solstice**.

An equinox happens twice a year. It's when the length of day and night is almost equal. A solstice also occurs twice a year. It's marked by the longest and shortest days.

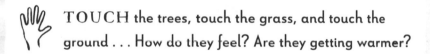

TOUCH the trees, touch the grass, and touch the ground . . . How do they feel? Are they getting warmer?

spring
showers

Splashing around in nature

Spring is famous for its showers. So next time it rains, grab a raincoat and some boots and run outside . . . Hold your arms out wide and open your palms toward the sky. Can you catch the raindrops on your tongue?

Splash in some puddles! Jump, tap, and dance in the rain! Can you make a splashing tune, or create some rhythms and beats with your dancing feet?

Do your very own rain dance and perhaps sing a rain song too!

♡ How does dancing in the rain make you FEEL?

2. High up in the air where it's cold, the fine vapor **condenses** into little water droplets to make clouds.

WHERE DOES RAIN COME FROM?

Rain falls from the sky— but how and why? On Earth, water is constantly moving and recycling over and over again in a WATER CYCLE.

1. Water that is warmed by the sun **evaporates**, floating up into the air as misty **water vapor.**

3. Once a cloud becomes too heavy, water falls from it as rain, snow, or hail. This is called **precipitation.**

catch the rain

Make your own rain gauge

Spring is a very rainy time of year! Find out just how much rain is falling in your area by making a rain gauge and keeping a weather journal.

WHAT YOU NEED:

- an empty 2-liter plastic bottle
- scissors
- modeling clay
- sticky tape
- ruler
- notebook and pencil

1. Ask an adult to cut around the plastic bottle about two thirds up from the bottom.

2. Stick a layer of modeling clay into the bottom of the bottle to create a flat base for your measurements.

TIP *use the rainwater you collect to water plants.*

3. Turn the top of the bottle upside down and fix it inside the bottom part using sticky tape. This will act as a funnel for the rain.

4. Place your rain gauge in an uncovered area outside.

5. Check your rain gauge at the same time every day and use a ruler to measure the amount of rainwater that has collected, in inches. Empty out any water once you've finished.

TIP *bury your rain gauge a little way down into the ground or stack some stones around it to stop it blowing over in the wind.*

6. Start a weather journal to keep track of your measurements.

chasing
rainbows

How rainbows appear in the sky

Now the sky changes, bruised by the promise of rain. Drops fall and soft splashes darken the earth.

The spring shower hasn't stopped when the sun emerges from behind a cloud and warms the air.

Keeping the sun behind you, look up at the sky. What can you see?

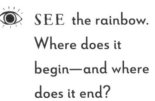 SEE the rainbow. Where does it begin—and where does it end?

How many colors can you count?

High above, through the curtain of rain, a splash
of colors arcs across the sky. It's a rainbow!
As the sunshine passes through the
raindrops, they reveal the
color spectrum that
light contains.

RED
ORANGE
YELLOW
GREEN
BLUE
INDIGO
VIOLET

LISTEN to the sky.
What sounds can you hear?

LEARN Rainbows in the
sky are formed when sunlight
passes through rain.

marvelous mud!

A poem to read in rain boots

Mushy and muddy or squashy and scoopy,
mud is just lovely because it's so gloopy!

Oozing and squelchy or stuck-in-the mucky,
mud can be belchy and pat-a-cake yucky!

Dig in the dirt, find a big stick to mix it,
now water it, shape it, then bake it to fix it.

Down in the earth all the worms underground,
are turning and churning to move it around.

Pushing through mush with a squash and a shove,
earthworms are munching the mud that they love!

Oozing and squashy it's lovely and muddy
cooling and mushy—oh mud is my buddy!

What does mud feel like to TOUCH?

messing
around

A world made of mud

You can squish it, dig it, pile it, push it, make handprints with it, jump in it, slide in it, and mush it . . . There are so many things you can do with the stuff that makes our world!

Wet mud is soft but what happens when it's dry?
Make a cake of mud and bake it in the sun to find out.

Can you make a pattern of muddy handprints?
Or just enjoy feeling the mud between your fingers—or toes!

Can you describe
the SMELL
of mud?

Who lives in mud?
EARTHWORMS!

These eyeless, squashy gardeners breathe through
their skin and need to keep it moist, so they love to
live in damp earth. They wiggle their pink, muscly
bodies to push through the soil, munching mud
and pooping it out again as they go. When spring
arrives, worms get busy as the soil softens.

 Just BE . . . a worm. Watch
how they wiggle and join in!

49

for a
rainy day

Pebble painting

This activity is perfect for a rainy spring day when you're stuck inside. To prepare in advance, look out for stones at the beach or in wooded areas, parks, or gardens.

WHAT YOU NEED:

- a selection of smooth stones or pebbles
- acrylic paints
- paintbrushes
- a cup of water, to clean brushes
- old newspaper or a craft mat

1. Wash your stones thoroughly and allow to dry before painting.

2. Protect the table or surface where you will be painting with old newspaper or a craft mat.

Here are some ideas to get you started:

- Spring flowers
- Lambs
- Chicks
- A rainbow
- A tree covered in blossoms

TIP *You might want to paint your stone all one color first and let it dry before adding extra details on top.*

3. Get creative! Paint your stones with pictures and designs that remind you of spring!

TIP *Think about the shape of your stone. Does it remind you of anything that you could turn it into?*

treasure
hunt

Searching for signs of spring

There are many treasures waiting to be found in spring. Next time you plan a trip to the park, woods, or a green space near where you live, look out for the following . . .

A PEBBLE to hold. Rough or smooth? Describe how it feels!

A PUDDLE to jump in. Does it make a good splash?

A FLOWER to smell. Describe its scent. What does it look like? Draw it!

A FEATHER to find. What bird does it come from?

TIP *You could also make your own treasure hunt by taking some painted pebbles (pages 50–51) with you and hiding them for your friends to find!*

A BUG to watch. How does it move? What is it?

A TWIG to carry. Does it have buds and leaves?

A BIRD to listen to. Can you hear their song? Can you identify them?

A BEE to see and hear. What is it doing?

A CATKIN to touch. How does it feel? Does it have a perfume?

A NEW SHOOT to look at. How many leaves does it have?

what is spring?

A poem to read in the wild

What is the color of spring?
The greenest green of little leaf
The creeping roots of underneath
the tiny green of grassy shoots,
or mossy green of muddy boots!

In every shade, in every hue
Of every other color, too . . .
Oh hello yellow, pink, and blue!

A rainbow over everything
In every color of the spring!

What sounds can you hear in spring?
The belch of frog, the squelch of mud
The splash of rivers in the flood
A scudding cloud across the sky
A chorus every dawn will cry,

"It's coming—listen, look, and see
The peeping buds upon the tree!
The flowers growing wild and free!"

The sound of spring in everything!

What perfumes can you smell in spring?
The budding blooms of every flower
Raindrops falling in a shower
Damp of grass, and silver bark
The muddy puddles in the park!

Inhale the air, the scent of spring
and smell the new in everything!

What does spring feel like?
Like stretching tall, like waking up
Like drinking from a cooling cup.

The tenderness of everything
The soft and gentle breath of spring
The sunny glow, the growing calm
The smoothest pebble in my palm . . .

The fluffy tails on pussy willow
falling in a furry pillow!

As rooted as the tallest tree
I feel the spring in all I see
in every living thing, like me.

All senses stirring in the spring
"Wake up! Wake up!" she seems to sing,
"And find the lovely things I bring!"

be prepared

Tips for the outdoors

What to pack
The weather in spring can change a lot! Check the weather forecast before you head out to help you choose what to wear and pack.

Top tips:

- Even on sunny days, it is best to be prepared! Pack a raincoat and a warm sweater in case the weather changes.

- Pack a spare pair of socks and pants in case you get soggy!

Rain boots or hiking boots

Raincoat

Sweater or fleece

Waterproof pants or overalls

Notebook and pencil

Stay safe

- Never touch or pick plants without permission from an adult.

- Foraging for food can be fun, but don't eat anything you find outdoors unless an adult tells you it's safe.

- Make sure an adult always knows where you are and don't wander off alone.

- Be careful near ponds, rivers, and lakes. Don't go in the water without an adult nearby.

Respect wildlife

- Try to leave nature as you found it.
- Put your trash in a trash can, or take it home with you.
- Try not to disturb wild animals.
- Don't touch nests.

Backpack

Water bottle

Sunscreen

Sun hat

Snacks

field notes

Recording spring's changes

Keeping a nature journal or scrapbook is a fun and creative way to appreciate nature and track the changing seasons. Here are some ideas to get you started:

- Draw and paint.

- Press leaves and flowers between journal pages.

- Make rubbings—leaves, bark, and rocks work well!

- Write your own spring poems.

- Keep a weather journal—have you checked your rain gauge today? (see pages 42–43)

- Include photographs you've taken in nature.

- Track a plant's growth by measuring it regularly with a ruler.

  - Make a note of the animals and plants you spot. Can you identify them all?

    - Once you've identified an animal or plant, keep a tally of how many you see.

Observation notes

Here are some questions to ask yourself when you spot
an animal or plant:

1. What color is it?

2. What shape and size is it?

3. What would it feel like to touch?

4. Does it have a smell?

5. What sound does it make?

spring words

amphibians
Cold-blooded animals that don't have scales. They can live in water and on land.

bud
A young part of a plant that opens up into a flower or leaf.

camouflage
Something that looks like its surroundings to blend in or hide.

catkin
A long, thin cluster of tiny flowers that hangs from the branches of a tree.

color spectrum
The 7 colors found in light that the human eye can see: red, orange, yellow, green, blue, indigo, and violet. These are also the colors in a rainbow.

condenses
When water vapor (see next page) cools and turns into droplets of water. You often see it form on cold glasses or windows.

equinox
An event that happens twice a year where day and night are almost the same length.

evaporates
When water turns into water vapor (see opposite). This makes it look as if the water has disappeared, like when a puddle dries up.

forage
When a person or animal wanders around looking for food.

froglet
A tiny frog that has recently developed from a tadpole.

frogspawn
Clear little balls that look like jelly and contain frog's eggs.

germination
When a new plant starts to grow from a seed.

mammals
Animals that breathe air, grow hair, have a backbone, and feed their young milk.

metamorphosis
When an animal changes its form as it grows, transforming into something completely different. An example of metamorphosis is a tadpole growing into a frog.

precipitation
When liquid or solid water falls from the clouds as rain, snow, or hail.

solstice
There are two solstices every year. The summer solstice is the longest day of the year, when Earth is tilted closest to the sun. The winter solstice is the shortest day, when Earth is tilted furthest away from the sun.

tadpole
A small, young animal with gills and a long tail that lives in water and will grow into an adult frog.

water vapor
Water that is in the form of a gas and appears invisible.

waterbird
Birds that live on or around water.

wetland
Wet areas of land, including marshes, bogs, and swamps.

index

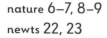

GABBY DAWNAY

Gabby is the author of over 20 books for children, a regular contributor to *OKIDO* magazine and a scriptwriter for children's television.

DORIEN BROUWERS

Dorien is an award-winning illustrator and author. She started writing and illustrating picture books as a gift for her son.

LOUISE BLACK

Louise is a Deputy Headteacher, and holds a Level 3 Forest School Leader qualification. She supports providing outdoor learning for all children.